ELEMENTS OF THE **EXTRAORDINARY**

Tea Leaves, Herbs, and Flowers

Fortune-telling the Gypsy Way!

ELEMENTS OF THE **EXTRAORDINARY**

Tea Leaves, Herbs, and Flowers

Fortune-telling the Gypsy Way!

GILLIAN KEMP

Illustrated by Mary Kuper

ELEMENT
CHILDREN'S BOOKS

SHAFTESBURY, DORSET · BOSTON, MASSACHUSETTS · MELBOURNE, VICTORIA

To my favorite children,
goddaughter Samantha Kemp and her sister Lauren Kemp.
Goddaughter Katy Cody and her sister Louisa Cody,
Edward and Rupert Swift,
and all children everywhere,
including you.

© Element Children's Books 1998
Text © Gillian Kemp 1998
Illustrations © Mary Kuper 1998

First published in Great Britain in 1998 by Element Children's Books
The Old School House, Bell Street, Shaftesbury, Dorset SP7 8BP

Published in the USA in 1998 by Element Books Inc.
160 North Washington Street, Boston, MA 02114

Published in Australia in 1998 by Element Books Limited
and distributed by Penguin Books Australia Ltd
487 Maroondah Highway, Ringwood, Victoria 3134

British Library Cataloging in Publication data available.
Library of Congress Cataloging in Publication data available.

ISBN 1-901881-92-X

Cover design by Ness Wood
Cover photography by Jon Stone

Typeset by Dorchester Typesetting Group Ltd
Printed and bound in Great Britain by Creative Print and Design

Contents

Magic, Mystery, and Gypsy Fortune-telling

When you are young you have so much future ahead of you that you dream of romance, success, friendships, and travel to exotic places. Will such dreams ever come true?

Surprisingly, the answer may be found in tea leaves. The Romanies, or Gypsies, a race of nomads who spread around the world from India, were masters of the art of reading the future in tea leaves. By revealing their secrets, this book tells you everything you need to know so that you, too, can read fortunes, predict the future, and pass messages to your friends using secret signs called *patrin*, and *rosalo-jib*, the Romany language of flowers.

When Gypsies first arrived in Britain they lived in tents called *benders* which they made by bending nine long green sticks into a semi-circle and covering them with blankets. For centuries, Gypsies slept in such tents and cooked on

campfires. During the nineteenth
century they started to live
and travel in horse-drawn
caravans. Some of these
were like miniature Renais-
sance palaces, beautifully
painted and carved with
vine leaves, grapes, fruit,
horses, and the heads of
lions. Richer Romanies embellished their *vardos*, as they
called their caravans, with gold leaf. As recently as your
grandmother's time, these colorful vans were often seen in
towns, villages, and country lanes all over Britain.

The caravans had a door at the front. There was a wood-
burning stove inside, and built across the back of the caravan was a bed which could be pulled out to become a
double bed. Underneath the bed was a blanket cupboard in
which the children slept with the doors open. The caravans
were really bedrooms on wheels. Romanies worked and
cooked outdoors.

Unfortunately, most of these wonderful caravans have
been destroyed by a Romany ritual. When an owner of one
died, it was the custom to burn the caravan and all its
contents.

Romany Secret Signs

Because Romanies could neither read nor write they used
secret signs, which they called *patrin*, to let their friends or
family know which road they had taken. These signs are
still used and understood by Romanies worldwide.

☛ Although the caravan left wheel tracks, a Romany man might also leave a trail of wood shavings or peg chippings along the road he took. At crossroads or a fork he would indicate his direction by digging out a big clump of grass from the verge and leaving it beside the road he had taken.

☛ When Romanies moved on from a campsite, the ashes of their fire would reveal how long ago they had left. But, to give more precise information to their friends, they might leave a long branch, crossed by a shorter stick, pointing in

the direction they had taken. Some of them placed a branch in the ground with the bark peeled at one end. By feeling how dry the peeled part of the stick was, a Romany would know how long ago the party had left.

☛ By leaving on the ground a long stick to represent each man, a shorter stick to symbolize each woman, and twigs or sprigs of heather for each child, Romanies showed how many of each had left the site to travel on.

☛ A rag tied to a hedge indicated that the nearest house was worth calling at. Two rags meant Romanies would *not* be made welcome.

Romany Ramble

It would be fun while on a country ramble with friends for two of you to go ahead leaving a Romany trail. Ten minutes later, the others follow the signs to catch up.

Language, and Life on the Roads

Because Romanies originated in India, they are usually dark-skinned and dark-haired. Worldwide, they speak a language called *Romanes* which has its roots in an ancient and sacred Indian language called *Sanskrit*. Romanes also borrows from the European languages of the countries through which the Romanies travel. Romanes has been passed down by word of mouth from one Romany generation to another. Romanies preserved their history through their oral tradition of storytelling but not in writing.

Romanies arrived in Europe nine centuries ago, wearing colorful costumes and bearing aristocratic names. Tribal elders called themselves *dukes of little **Egypt*** which is where the word Gypsy comes from. Romanies probably set foot in Britain long before the Lord High Treasurer of Scotland first noted their arrival there in 1505.

The men earned a living as tinsmiths, coppersmiths,

blacksmiths, and horse dealers. Some worked seasonally as casual farm laborers, picking fruit, vegetables, and hops. The women weaved baskets, carved pegs, and fascinated people by reading their palms and telling their fortunes using cards or by gazing into a crystal ball.

It was the women who usually made house calls to sell pegs, lace, flowers, and lucky charms such as fossils, shells, and coral. If given a cup of tea, they also offered to read the householder's fortune in the tea leaves.

Romanies developed the art of tea-leaf reading in their tea-growing homeland, India. The custom of tea-leaf reading spread with the Romanies as they traveled to the West.

No one drank tea in Britain until the seventeenth century. At that time tea was very expensive, costing £3 per pound (just under half a kilo) and was possessively hoarded by the rich. British India began to export tea in 1840. By the end of the nineteenth century, both Chinese and Indian tea became affordable to most people in England.

Romanies have been referred to as the *last Victorians* because of their fastidiousness and strict courtship rites. The Romany word for uncleanliness is *mockadi*, similar to the slang word *muckety*. Romanies think it *mockadi* that some house dwellers wash their clothes together with tea towels and table linen.

Nowadays, because of their nomadic lifestyle, and to prevent themselves from getting ill, Romanies always take with them a series of stainless steel bowls. Each one is used only for a specific everyday chore, such as washing vegetables, washing meat, doing the dishes, washing clothes; and one is used for washing tablecloths and tea towels. They have another bowl or two for washing themselves. Romanies consider it extremely *mockadi* to use the wrong bowl.

Romanies have always kept themselves apart from the rest of society, even though many have now intermarried. Courting was not easy because parents were strict and wanted their children to marry other Romanies.

The Language of Flowers

In their tight-knit but mobile society the Romanies had plenty of time, as they journeyed hundreds of miles, to observe the many different varieties of plants along the way. They gave them names and invented a language which used flowers as symbols. Eventually, the meaning of flowers became as important to them as reading tea leaves.

Rosalo-jib, the Romany language of flowers, is rooted in the Orient but blossomed in Europe during the eighteenth and nineteenth centuries. Romanies lived closer to nature than anyone else and developed the language of flowers as they traveled. Flowers spoke volumes in delicate situations in which their code of behavior precluded an open expression of feelings.

Because Romanies could neither read nor write, they

wrote no love letters. They had to say it all with flowers. Today, like campfire smoke, many flower meanings have disappeared into thin air. But many traces remain and have been absorbed into our own traditions, such as the gift of a red rose meaning *I love you.*

Gypsy Fortune-telling

The Romany secrets of tea-leaf reading will be revealed in the next chapter, but before you begin a session of fortune-telling, surprise your friends with your amazing knowledge of Romany folklore. First, tell them about these exciting people who came from the East wearing colorful clothes, telling strange tales, and weaving wonderful spells with their fortune-telling. Your friends will soon be under your spell.

Now it's time to set out on your exciting trail of the Romany Gypsies. Read on for romance and a lot of fun.

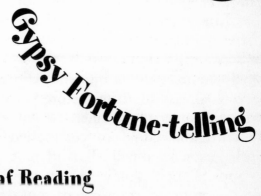

CHAPTER 2

Gypsy Fortune-telling

Romany Tea-leaf Reading
Mutterimengri Dukkeripen

Like all things magical, reading tea leaves is shrouded in mystery. Romanies believe a tea drinker's *aura*, the subtle personal feeling that emanates from and surrounds each of us, remains in the cup for a while after drinking.

They say the electrical vibration of the aura, which in religious art is shown as a halo around the head, is intensified in the tea leaves and an even stronger impression is made if, while drinking, a person concentrates on what he or she wishes to know.

The excitement begins when you invite your closest friends around for tea so that you can read their leaves and reveal their future, their hopes, and their desires.

ᴈᴗ Prepare the scene by laying out white cups and saucers (not mugs). Get a teapot and a packet of loose tea. Large-leaf tea brews the best imagery. Tea bag tea is too powdery. You'll also need some milk.

ᴈᴗ When your friends arrive, make the tea by first warming the pot with boiling water. Empty the teapot and place in it one heaped teaspoonful of tea for each friend, plus one extra for the pot. Boil enough water to fill the pot and pour it over the tea.

ᴈᴗ Leave the tea to brew for three to five minutes. Pour a small amount of milk into each cup. Stir the tea in the pot in a clockwise direction before you pour it into the cups without using a tea-strainer.

ᴈᴗ When the tea is poured, the leaves in each person's cup will tell a different story.

ᴈᴗ **Surface bubbles** indicate money.

ᴈᴗ **A floating tea leaf** is an omen of a letter in the post.

ᴈᴗ **A floating twig** augurs a visitor. If the twig is small, the visitor will be a child. To find out whether your visitor will be male or female, bite the stick. If it is soft it represents a woman or girl. If hard, it indicates that a man or a boy will be calling on you.

ᴈᴗ To enquire on what day of the week the guest may arrive, place the twig on the back of your left hand. Next, call out the name of the current day and tap your wrist with your right hand, continuing with the following days of the week. The day called out as the twig drops off is the day you can expect a visitor.

ᴈᴗ As you drink every drop of the tea, concentrate on what

it is you want to know. The person whose cup is being read should lift the cup into the air, swirl it three times in a wide anti-clockwise circular motion before placing the cup upside-down on the saucer.

❧ After a few seconds, the tea-leaf reader lifts the cup and allows his or her imagination to run freely on the shapes and patterns that have been formed by the tea leaves. The patterns formed on the saucer can then be read.

What Tea Leaves Can Tell You

❧ **Leaves close to the cup handle** represent events close to home.

❧ **Leaves to the left of the handle** show events from the past.

❧ **Leaves to the right of the handle** depict events in the immediate future.

❧ **Leaves at the rim** foretell future destiny.

❧ **Leaves at the bottom of the cup** represent events that will occur in the distant future.

❧ **Dark-colored leaves** represent men and boys, as well as people with dark hair.

❧ **Light-colored leaves** depict women and girls, and fair-haired people.

❧ **Tea leaf stalks** also indicate people. They will be dark or fair according to the lightness or darkness of the stalk's coloring.

❧ **Long, hard stalks** symbolize men.

❧ **Thin shorter stalks** symbolize women.

❧ **Erect stalks** denote friends.

❧ **Crossed stalks** predict enemies.

❧ **Slanting stalks** indicate vexation.

❧ **Groups of dots** are an omen of money.

❧ **Small single dots** represent letters.

❧ **A large dot** augurs a gift.

❧ **Squares** stand for peace and happiness.

❧ **Oblongs** mean quarrels.

❧ **Large unbroken circles** are a promise of happiness.

❧ **Snake-like lines** are lucky portents of good fortune. If they are surrounded by small dots, a windfall of money or an increase of cash can be expected.

❧ **Straight lines** predict new enterprises.

❧ **Letters of the alphabet** represent the initial of a person's name, or a place, or maybe a month.

❧ **Numbers** formed by tea leaves can be taken literally to indicate things such as the day of the week or month, as well as referring to a number of people or objects. But they also have the following symbolic meanings:

1 ❧ Expect happy days ahead.

2 ❧ A pleasant event will soon occur twice.

3 ❧ Your wish will soon come true.

4 ❧ You will be successful in school.

5 ❧ A marvelous surprise is on its way to you.

6 ❧ Everyone you meet will like you.

7 ❧ You will achieve your ambition.

8 ❧ A minor disappointment will make you stronger.

9 ❧ Promise of bright and happy days ahead.

The shapes formed by tea leaves each have a particular meaning. As you stare into a tea cup you will be surprised at how easily distinguishable some shapes are. It sounds peculiar, but it may be easier to recognize shapes if you half close your eyes.

Of course, real-life things will not be accurately represented but the tea leaves will form shapes that resemble them. The more fertile the tea-leaf reader's imagination is, the more easily discernible the images will be. Children are especially good at reading tea leaves because they have a more fluid imagination than adults.

Just as other children learn to read and write, Romany children, particularly girls, begin learning how to read tea leaves at the age of five or six. It is simple groundwork for the other forms of divination that Romany children will also be taught.

Tea-leaf reading is one of the easiest ways to tell fortunes and the more you do it, the better at it you will become. Once people know you read the tea cups, almost everyone you meet will want you to read theirs. Everybody will want you at their party. It will make you popular for the rest of your life.

Tea leaves in a cup are really just a way to focus your *clairvoyant* powers. Clairvoyance is the ability to see in your mind people and incidents which are distant in both time and place. The Romanies say that interpreting the leaves will enhance your intuition (understanding from within).

By practicing tea-leaf divination your psychic soul and mind will develop and become stronger. Being psychic means you are sensitive to spiritual influences because your spirit is linked into spiritual energy that is all around you and is part of you. Being psychic means you feel or sense that something in particular will happen.

Guardian Angels

If you feel nervous about making the correct predictions when you read a person's tea cup, you could say a silent prayer to your guardian angel while your friend is drinking his or her tea. The same can be said if you are reading your own fortune in a tea cup.

Like everyone, you have your own personal angel whose job is to help you through life from birth to death. Because your angel is linked from heaven to you, he or she, by divine intervention, will put the right thoughts into your head so that you say the right things during a reading. When looking into a tea cup, it's best to say the first thing that springs into your mind.

It is very important to silently thank your angel when you have finished giving your reading. Saying thank you closes the psychic door which you opened with your little prayer. It is rather like opening the front door of your home. It would be dangerous to leave the door wide open day and night, because you would not have control over what came in or went out. Similarly, it would be foolish to turn on the kitchen tap and not turn it off again. You must close, or turn off, whatever you have opened.

Heaven works with you when you ask, and protects you when you have finished.

Secrets of Gypsy Fortune-telling

The following *A–Z of Tea-leaf Symbols* will reveal what is meant by the images you may see in a tea cup. You can turn the cup to look at the tea leaves from any angle. If you glance into the cup from different directions some shapes may look like more than one symbol but a story of the future will begin to emerge as you link together all the images you see.

A-Z of Tea-leaf Symbols

ACORN

The seed of an oak tree seen in a tea cup is a very good sign. It reveals the fulfillment of ambitions. Perhaps more pocket money will follow. If you are worried about someone's health, the acorn is to reassure you that he or she will soon recover.

Romany girls and women are superstitious about acorns which they say are sacred to the Goddess of Nature. They carry or wear an acorn as an amulet in an attempt to stay young.

A Romany girl who wishes to speed the return of her lover will sleep with an acorn under her pillow.

ACROBAT

A balancing figure is a sign to be strong. Do not allow anyone to toss your emotions to and fro.

AIRPLANE or AEROPLANE

You may travel abroad if the plane is heading away from the handle of the cup. But you can expect an overseas visitor if the plane is facing towards it. If family members have overseas business connections, they may soon travel by air.

ALLIGATOR

Keep alert. Someone may try to trick you.

ALPS

The message given by a range of mountains is that you should aim high. If you cultivate your special talents, you will reach life's dizzy heights of success. In the near future, you may go on holiday where there are mountains.

ANCHOR

You will be riding the waves of success. Your wishes will come true. An ambition anchored on dedication will secure the firm foundation you need to build on.

ANT

You will be busy working on a new project or revising for exams. If there are lots of ants, just do your best and do not get *ants in your pants* by worrying.

The Romanies do not step on ants or destroy a colony of them, because they believe that a nest close to home is a sign of future wealth. Lots of ants, they say, are a sign that it will rain.

ANTELOPE

You are surrounded by more tenderness and affection than you realize.

APE

An unruly acquaintance is probably best kept at a distance. Do not get involved.

APPLE

A promise of love. Well deserved rewards. You may win a contest.

There is more to the saying, *an apple a day keeps the doctor away*, than you may think. Romanies say an apple represents eternal youth. Gambling Romany men count pips in the apple and bet on the total number.

APRON

You or someone close may be cooking a special meal for a memorable occasion, perhaps your mother's birthday.

Traditionally, Romany women wear aprons. If a girl loses her apron, it is a sign that her lover is thinking of her. If he wipes his hands on her apron he will fall helplessly in love with her. Romanies say the wearer can expect marriage and a baby within 12 months if her apron falls off.

ARCH

An arch heralds the beginning of a bright new era for you. Life is going to change for the better. If you find yourself in a building with an arch, fate will be about to give you a helping hand.

To alleviate whooping cough, boils, blackheads, and rheumatism, Romanies walk through an arch of brambles. They believe the complaint gets symbolically caught on the thorns and is left behind them.

ARM

Help is at hand to give the support you need. But, if there is someone you feel should be kept at arm's length, follow your instincts, and avoid risks.

ARROW

An arrow pointing towards the rim of a cup means good news is on its way. If it is pointing away from the rim, you will be spreading cheerful news to others. Any other direction an arrow faces is telling you to head for your target like an arrow because you are going to achieve your aim.

AXE

An axe is a symbol of power and light. Someone or something may have to be axed from your life if you want to continue progressing.

BABY

You may hear news of someone in the family, or perhaps a neighbor, expecting a baby.

The Romanies say that when a baby travels for the first time its journey must be uphill as a sign that it will do well in life.

BAG

Someone will give you a present.

BAGPIPES

Avoid arguments and discord.

BALL

Grasp an opportunity with both hands. You are going to have good fun and may be a person who enjoys football or is connected to the sport. You will make the team, know someone in it, or may be invited to watch a match.

BALLOON

A balloon represents a party invitation. A hot-air balloon symbolizes that you will rise to a high status in life if you concentrate on your talent and rise above distractions.

BANANA

You are going to achieve an important position at school or in a club. A bunch of bananas indicates that you may find an overseas pen-pal.

BANNER

Through hard work you will make a name for yourself and receive rewards far beyond your expectations.

BASKET

You will have many opportunities to explore. A full basket reveals that you have lots of friends.

BAT

This nocturnal flying mammal is a lucky sign that implies someone will reveal an intimate secret to you.

The Romanies say bats flying in twilight, but earlier than usual, are a sign of good weather on its way.

BEAR

A bear in your cup reveals that you are strong-willed, so try not to irritate your parents who may currently have lost patience with you.

BED

If the bed looks unfamiliar, expect to go on holiday, away with your school, or perhaps to a *sleepover*. If the bed is disheveled, someone who has taken to his or her bed will recover. A neat bed signifies that great happiness will always be yours.

BEE

According to the Romanies, bees are fortune-tellers. A bee in your cup reveals that you can see the future better than you think. You may get a part-time job and become a *busy bee*.

If you see one bee, you may receive an increase in your pocket money.

A swarm of bees augurs a family wedding or baptism. A beehive means you may become involved in fund-raising, perhaps for a school fête or charity.

Romanies never kill bees. They will not even drive one away for fear of driving away good luck. Romanies say a bee indoors foretells the arrival of a visitor. A bee landing on your hand augurs that money will come to you. A bee flying around a sleeping child's head is an omen of a happy life.

BEETLE

This insect in a teacup means you may receive a small windfall of money.

Romanies have enormous respect for beetles and think that killing one is an invitation to misfortune.

BELL

A church bell means wedding bells will ring for someone you know. If it is a hand bell, you can expect good news that will ring in a change to good fortune.

The Romanies believe that to hear bells pealing is a sign that you will soon be going on a journey.

BICYCLE

You may be invited on an outing, a picnic, or a bike ride with friends. Perhaps you will get a new bike.

BIRD

A flying bird suggests someone will bring good news. A flock of birds augurs a trip abroad. A caged bird indicates obstructions, but you will quickly escape if the door is open. A bird holding something in its beak denotes a reconciliation after a quarrel.

A ring beside a bird foretells news of a marriage announcement.

Romanies say if you see a flock of birds flying on your right as you begin a journey, the trip will be successful. They also say it is lucky if a bird's dropping lands on you, because birds signify spiritual help.

BIRD'S NEST

A nest is a very good omen and indicates that you will be able to feather your nest. Your home life will be happy and comfortable. Perhaps you will help redecorate your room or move into another bedroom at home.

BOAT

A sea voyage or boat trip is denoted.

BOOK

An open book reveals you are much brighter than you think. You can become whatever you put your mind to being – so study hard. A closed book denotes the beginning of a new chapter in your life.

BOOMERANG

This is a little warning to be careful about what you say about other people, because gossip always bounces back.

BOOT

A boot pointing away from the handle of a teacup represents an exciting journey to somewhere you have never been before.

The superstitious Romanies say that a boot placed on a chair is a sign of a family quarrel.

BOTTLE

One bottle denotes a party. An image of several bottles represents medicine for an illness and can indicate recovery from an emotional upset. If a family member works on a milk round, he or she can expect good news.

BOWL OF FRUIT

Your activities will be fruitful. Fun and excitement will be plentiful in your life.

BOX

An open box means a gift or parcel will arrive. A small box suggests you will receive a present from a relative. A closed box means a mislaid item will be recovered.

BRANCH

A leafy branch symbolizes branching out in your academic studies and hobbies. It is also a sign of friendship that means you should give way or at least bend to parental advice.

BRIDGE

You may cross a bridge when you go somewhere. But, symbolically, you are crossing a bridge to a successful and happier life surrounded by friends.

BROOCH

This token of affection shows that someone is more fond of you than you realize. An initial nearby may reveal to you who it is.

BROOM

A household broom illustrates that it is time to make a clean sweep. A besom (a broom made of twigs) augurs that someone could be jumping the broomstick and tying a wedding knot.

The Welsh Gypsies often married by *broomstick weddings*. They said their vows and jumped over a branch of broom plant placed on the ground.

BUCKLE

You will make the right connections. Partnerships will be strengthened if a buckle appears.

BUGLE

A time of struggle and hard work will not go unnoticed nor unappreciated by your nearest and dearest.

BULL

 You may renew contact with an old friend or could form close ties with a Taurean person. Around the time of Taurus, 21 April-20 May, there may be a happy surprise for you.

BUOY
You will keep on top of school work and all that is demanded of you. You will float with ease through life.

BUTTERCUP
You will attract riches. Summer will be playful.

BUTTERFLY

An enchanting situation will present itself during a light-hearted day out. Someone may flirt with you. Your gift of understanding spiritual matters may bring you pleasure and notoriety because a butterfly is symbolic of the soul and of an unconscious attraction towards the light. A wish made when you see the first butterfly of summer is said to come true. These *flying-flowers*, being also a sign of wealth, are never trapped or killed by Romanies.

CABBAGE
A cabbage is not just a sign that you should *eat your greens because they are good for you*. It also means you will be given permission to do something you have been longing to do.

Many Gypsies have earned a seasonal living by picking fruit and vegetables. They believe a *double* cabbage, one that has two shoots from a single root, is a lucky omen.

CABIN

A cabin offers shelter and a retreat from boredom. It is a good time to organize a weekend away with friends.

CACTUS

When put to the test, you will surprise yourself with the reserves of energy you have.

CAGE

One of your pets may need some more attention or a visit to the vet.

CAKE

Seeing a cake in the tea leaves means there will soon be a birthday party, either at your home or a friend's.

CALENDAR

You will be putting important dates in your diary. Perhaps you should begin writing a diary.

CAMEL

Camels have great endurance. Seeing one in the tea leaves means help will come whenever you need it.

CAMPFIRE

A campfire scene in your cup means you will always be rich in friendships.

Romanies have a code never to walk in front of anyone sitting at a campfire. No Gypsy must ever poke another's fire until they have known one another for at least seven years. Ivy is never burned because woodland spirits may be hiding in the evergreen leaves. Romanies never light a fire in the same place twice because it is considered unlucky. They say the best place to light a fire is by a hedge where it will be sheltered from the wind, and therefore will burn less wood.

Christmas Eve, New Year's Eve, and Midsummer Night's Eve are three nights of the year when Romanies never let the campfire go out, because that would mean their luck is running out. Men traditionally gather firewood and light the campfire, but women keep it alight while the men are absent. If a fire suddenly flares up brightly when a woman pokes it she will expect her husband to return in a cheerful mood.

CANDLE

There will always be light in your life. You can expect good news. Love and inspiration will be yours.

If a candle refuses to be lit Romanies think it means that rain will fall. A bright spark in a candle augurs good news. If the wick sparks, strangers will arrive.

CANNON

Someone you know may join the armed forces. You may hear news of someone in the forces or visit a military base.

CAP

Beware of someone you trust. This is not a good time for telling your secrets.

CAR

You or someone close to you may pass a driving test, have the car serviced, or even buy a new car. You may travel by car to somewhere unusual.

CART

Financial success is assured by the symbol of a cart in your teacup.

CASTLE

Castles you build in the air can become reality. Such imaginings are sometimes forerunners of what you are destined to be. Have faith in your dreams is the message in a castle.

CAT

A cat is a symbol of good luck and domestic bliss, except when it is pouncing because that denotes trickery. You may be fortunate, have *nine lives* like a cat, and expect to land on your feet in tricky situations. You could acquire a cat or care for the neighbors' cat while they are away.

It is very lucky to see a black cat cross your path. Romanies say a cat sneezing is an omen of good fortune coming into the home. But if it sneezes three times a family member will catch a cold. It is a sign of a downpour if a cat washes its ears, but of only a shower if it licks its tail.

Windy weather is augured if a cat rushes around a room, clawing furnishings. To have a strange cat wander into your home heralds good fortune.

CAULDRON

Life becomes magical. You may cultivate a healthy new wholefood diet or become a good cook.

CHAIR

An empty chair augurs a visitor.

Romanies say if a person knocks a dining chair over after a meal it means he or she has lied while eating.

CHERRIES

Happy summer days are forecast by one or more cherries. You may also expect your first taste of romance.

CHERUB

You are blessed by heavenly help.

CHESSMEN

Your powers of concentration will increase with your efforts. You are acquiring a new skill.

CHILD

You will be enjoying light-hearted company and may be asked to help with a child.

CHIMNEY

You will have a secure home life. But if the chimney is ruined your hopes and dreams may be temporarily delayed.

CHURCH

A church is a sign that you should keep faith in a worrying or lonely situation. But it may also mean that you attend church or will join a church-related club.

CIRCLE

Because a circle looks like a wedding ring it sometimes heralds news of a wedding. But it also foretells complete success with your future plans.

CLOCK

A clock means it is time to prepare for your future. But you may give or receive a clock, or need to set your alarm for an early start to a special day.

CLOUDS

Clouds reveal that your troubles are evaporating. What happened was simply a storm in a teacup.

CLOVER

This lucky emblem symbolizes that you will *be in clover* and will do well for yourself.

Romanies place a four-leaf clover in their hat or button-hole to increase their intuition.

COAT

You will soon be dressing to go somewhere special.

COMPASS

A possible house or school move. You may change class, or soon be making new choices in your academic subjects.

CROOK

A shepherd's crook symbolizes protection and help from an adult, as well as divine power inspiring your own beliefs.

CROSS

You may be at a crossroads in life. Think carefully before making a decision.

CROWN

All your efforts will be crowned with success because you will have spiritual enlightenment. You may attend a May fair.

CUP

Your cup of happiness will be full. Reading tea leaves could become more than just a hobby – you may even earn a living by it.

CUPID

A highly emotional Valentine's card or love letter may arrive.

DANCER

A wish will come true if a dancer appears in your teacup. If dancing is your forte, the message is to keep on dancing – one day it may be your career.

DEER
You are loved and protected by your parents.

DESK
Your school report will be better than you think.

DIAMOND
A diamond shape denotes that you will receive a gift of jewelry.

DICE
Avoid taking a gamble or any kind of risk. Play safely.

DOG
You are surrounded by good friends. A dog at the bottom of the cup means a friend may call for your support.

Romanies believe that if a strange dog wanders into your home, you will gain a new friend. To meet a black and white or a spotted dog on a journey is a sign of a lucky day, and also of good news when you return home. Romanies say dogs not only see ghosts but can tell whether someone is good or bad. They react by wagging their tail or growling.

DOLL
A phase of light-hearted fun. Someone may give you a doll, a marionette, or a puppet.

DONKEY
You will need patience to overcome a disagreeable situation.

DOOR

The door to success is opening. You will meet important people who will help you to improve.

DRAGONFLY

Expect to be flitting around to accommodate a very welcome visitor.

DRESS

You will be buying a new outfit.

DRUM

Avoid any action that may begin a rumor.

DUCK

Luck, especially in spring, is forecast by a duck.

EAGLE

A sign that the best has yet to come. You will soar to great heights. Your father will give you a gift.

EAR

Expect to hear some good news.

About itching ears, Romanies say, *left for love, right for revenge*, or someone is speaking of you well or badly.

EARRINGS

Romanies say earrings are a sign that you are clairvoyant which means you will acquire special knowledge of things both seen and unseen.

Romanies pierce their ears in the belief that it will improve both their eyesight and their second sight (which is the ability to foresee the future).

EASEL

You have artistic flair, not necessarily with a paintbrush. Explore avenues with which you have an affinity.

EGG

A very good omen that promises success in a new project. You may hear of a baby's birth. Spring will be lucky for you.

ELF

Brilliant news out of the blue is going to add a sparkle to how you feel.

ENVELOPE

You will receive good news in a white envelope.

EYE

Someone whom you fear you may not see again will return. A person who is ill or injured will regain good health.

Romanies say it is an omen of good luck if your right eye becomes suddenly ticklish.

FACE

There will be an important meeting. Do not fear a test if you have one to face. Your chances of passing look promising. Many faces seen in the tea leaves predict a party, a fête, or a place where you will be among lots of people.

FAIRY

Spiritual power and protection are bringing you an enchanting life. Something magical may happen for you.

FEATHER

Since *birds of a feather flock together* is a saying the Romanies believe in, they maintain that a feather seen in a teacup foretells the appearance of someone who is destined to help you in life.

FEET

Your path through life may be extraordinary.

FIR TREE

Someone has everlasting love for you.

FIREPLACE

This is a sign of money coming into the home.

A Romany way to tell whether an absent family member is well and having good fortune is to poke a fire. If it burns brightly, the answer is *yes.*

Bright flames on one side forecast a wedding. Crackles are a sign of frost. Sparks flying indicate good news. Oval-shaped cinders denote news of a baby's birth.

FISH

 A sign of wisdom and knowledge, a fish signifies that time and tide are turning in your favor. Two fish can mean that a Piscean person will enter your life. The time of Pisces, 20 February–20 March, will be lucky for you.

FLOWER

One or more flowers in a cup are harbingers of good fortune. They reveal that you have many admirers and that your wishes may come true.

FONT

You may be invited to a baptism, but a font also means that an important new idea could come to you.

FOREST

There is the distinct possibility that you cannot see the wood for the trees. If this is the case, try looking at things long-term.

FOUNTAIN

You may hit the jackpot. Good fortune is flowing in your direction.

FOX

A lone fox means you are clever. Good fortune is in store. Be cautious and tread carefully.

Romanies say that it is lucky to see one fox in the wild.

FROG

This lucky sign augurs good health and happiness as well as changes for the better around the home.

Romanies avoid killing frogs. Because a frog's cry sounds similar to that of an injured child, they believe it would invite harm to one of their own children.

FRUIT

Fruitful activities will result from your earthly desires.

GALAXY

A galaxy of stars reveal you could find yourself mixing in star-studded company. Perhaps you will go to a show.

GARDEN
You will have happy days. Summer will be good.

GARLAND
If you see a garland of flowers, you can expect to receive congratulations, an award, or a certificate.

GARLIC
An image of garlic in your teacup is a sign that you have mystical powers.

GATE

A gate reveals that you will be expanding your horizons, leading away from obstructions to greater freedom and success.

GEESE
A childhood friend could become a life-long companion.

GIANT
Someone with a strong personality could have a big impact on you.

GLASS
A drinking glass means that you will be invited to a party.

GLOVE
You may be shaking hands with someone in a position of authority. You might get into the school or club you hope to.

If you drop a glove, get someone else to pick it up. That person will then have good luck.

GRAPES

Success is coming to you, but do not allow success to go to your head and intoxicate you.

GUITAR

If you are taking guitar lessons this is an omen that you should continue. It also means someone may pamper you.

HAMMOCK

This means you will soon be enjoying a well-deserved rest.

HAMPER

Life will feel like a picnic and you may go on one. Long-term, many good things lie in store for you.

HAND

A hand means your name will be on a list to join in a new activity that will help you in more ways than one.

The Romanies say an itching right palm is a sign that you will receive money. But you will spend money if your left hand itches.

HARP

A harp means you can expect your prayers to be answered.

HAT

You may hear someone's secret, keep it *under your hat*.

HAYSTACK

You will be reaping a harvest of good fortune. The summer months look promising.

HEART

A heart reveals that because you are kind-hearted you will attract love and affection from both people and animals. It also shows you will attain one of the greatest attributes of life – the capacity to be understanding and kind to people who are horrible to you.

HEATHER

A lucky emblem, promising happiness and good luck. You may win at something and achieve what you want.

Romanies say it is lucky to wear white heather. To see it growing is an omen of happiness. When Romanies marry they often wear white heather in their headdress.

HEDGEHOG

A hedgehog, or *hootchiwitchi* as the Romanies call it, is a sign of great happiness, especially during spring.

Romanies say hedgehogs are weather almanacs because they build the entrance to their nest facing away from whichever direction the wind is blowing.

HOLLY

A wish will be fulfilled during winter.

HORSE

This means you will travel far afield during your life.

Romanies, who like skewbald (brown and white) or piebald (black and white) horses, say that when horses stand with their backs to a hedge it is a sign of a storm brewing.

HORSESHOE

Good luck, your magical powers will not run out. If you ever find a horseshoe, you should pick it up and keep it as a good luck charm. It should be kept upright to keep the luck in.

HUMAN FIGURES

These represent people, perhaps those you know. An initial may be nearby. Their actions should help you to understand the meaning.

INITIALS

These represent the names of people or places. If initials spell a word, the Romanies say you will be rich.

INSECT

Something which may have been worrying you is not important. Stop worrying and be happy.

IRON

Life will run smoothly for you. You will never have a problem that you cannot cope with and solve.

IVY LEAF

You have sincere friends.

JACKET

You may be going on a shopping spree to buy new clothes.

JAGUAR

This animal reveals that you will quickly get what you want.

JESTER

You will be enjoying some fun and games somewhere special.

JUG

A friend will return something that belongs to you, but you may first have to remind him or her.

KETTLE

Domestic happiness is forecast. You will be entertaining at home, perhaps putting on the kettle to read tea leaves. You may be invited to read tea leaves to raise money.

KEY

An idea may dawn on you in a dream. It will suggest a new opportunity that will bring you success.

KING

An influential person will approach you with the intention of helping. He could be a private tutor.

KITE

You may receive a kite as a gift, fly one, or go to where there are kites. If you have a problem, you will soar above it.

KNIFE

A knife means that you can expect a male visitor to your home.

KNIGHT

Symbolically, a knight means that strength is on your side and that you are protected from harm.

LADDER

A ladder indicates that you are taking steps in the right direction to achieve a high position in life.

LADLE

You will be sharing pleasure with friends.

LADYBIRD

A ladybird is an omen of luck as well as a sign that you will become good at learning a foreign language.

Romanies say if a ladybird lands on your dress you will get a new one. The same goes for any other items on which a ladybird lands.

LAMB

A lamb symbolizes a happy year. When seen in a teacup, it is such a lucky sign that you should immediately make a wish.

LAMP

Light will be shed on a matter which has been confusing you.

LEAF

Good news. The more leaves the merrier, because every leaf represents a happy day in the future.

LETTER

You are about to receive good news that will make your parents proud of you.

LIGHTHOUSE

A lighthouse reveals that you will soon visit the coast.

LINES

In life, you have a clear path ahead.

LION

You will be mixing with important people. You may meet a Leo-born person. The time of Leo will be good for you, July 24 to August 23.

LIZARD

A warning not to panic but to sit tight. But a lizard is also a sign that you are good at sewing.

LOAF

A symbol that you will have plenty to live on. Alternatively, you may have to *use your loaf*, by thinking intelligently.

LUGGAGE

You may soon be packing for a journey.

MAGNET
Your optimism will attract good fortune.

MANSION
You may be visiting a mansion or grand house.

MAP
This reveals that you will be going somewhere you have never been before.

MAYPOLE
You may soon be mingling with new people who will make you happy. The month of May could be significant for the fulfillment of a wish.

MEDAL
You will achieve something you can feel pleased about. You may win a medal or certificate, or pass an exam.

MELON
Simply wait. Good fortune is about to land in your lap.

MIRROR

A hand mirror denotes that you are going to make a new friend. The happiness you give will be reflected back to you.

Romanies believe a person's reflection in a mirror is their soul, which is why they believe that to break a mirror will bring a curse of seven years of bad luck. The antidote is to put on a pair of gloves, collect the shattered glass in a handkerchief and bury it.

MISTLETOE

Someone has romantic designs on you.

MOLE

You could unearth some intriguing information.

Romanies say a mole consecutively sleeps for four hours and works for four hours and that you can set your watch by him. Underground, moles run as fast as a racehorse.

Romany mothers sometimes send their children to look for the fine earth that has been thrown up to the surface by moles. The earth is ideal for potting plants because the moles have sifted the soil in their search for worms to eat.

MONK

A monk seen in your tea leaves is said to reveal that you will acquire a deep spiritual knowledge.

MONKEY

A monkey is a sign that someone will be very embarrassed if you try to make him or her look silly.

MOON

To see the moon in a teacup not only reveals that you are clairvoyant but that great happiness is coming to you.

To increase your wealth, do as the Romanies do. When you see the new moon for the first time, turn your money over in your pocket. They also say a wish will be granted if you curtsy or bow to the New Moon.

Romany girls use the first new moon of the year to predict when they will marry. They hold a silk handkerchief to their eyes and through it they count the number of moons that appear to be reflected in a pond, a river, or even in a bucket of water. The total number of moons seen is the number of years they will wait before marriage.

MOTH

A moth reveals that you will be enjoying an evening out.

Romanies say that if a moth flies at you, important news will soon follow. White moths especially are omens of good luck.

MOUSE

A mouse in a teacup is a sign that someone who is unwell will recover their health.

MUSHROOM

A home in the country is revealed by a mushroom. You will soon be visiting someone there.

NAIL

A masonry nail is a lucky sign. If you find a nail, pick it up and take it home or carry it in your purse. A rusty nail is particularly lucky.

A Romany remedy to take sickness away is to wind a hair from an ill person's head around a nail. The nail is then driven into the ground or a post.

NECKLACE

A necklace reveals that you have many admirers. Someone may give you a necklace.

NEEDLE

People will speak highly of you. You may excel in needlecraft.

Romanies say that to break a needle when sewing is a sign of a wedding. To tangle the thread on a needle while stitching is an omen of good health. But if the thread gets itself into a knot there will be a quarrel.

NUMBERS

These can represent a number of days, the month, or date of the month when events will occur. But they also have symbolic meanings (see page 16).

NUN

A nun seen in the tea leaves shows that you have a good female friend.

NURSE

You may be seeing a nurse or visiting a hospital. But, you might also consider nursing as your vocation.

NUT

This is a prophecy of a pleasant surprise in store for you. It is also a sign that a wish may be granted.

NUTCRACKERS

You will crack a difficult situation and have a brilliant success.

OAK

An oak is a very lucky love emblem, whether a tree or a leaf. It reveals that you are surrounded by strong love.

OAR

This is a sign that you may expect a phase of hard work, but it will be followed by fun.

OCTOPUS

An octopus means that you should avoid the temptation to get caught up in something which you may regret.

ONION

An onion is a portent of such great happiness that others may be jealous of you.

The Romanies say if an onion that you have dug from your own garden has a thin skin it is a forecast of a mild winter.

OWL

An owl is a particularly lucky image to see. You already have strong powers of prophecy and wisdom but your intuition will grow in strength.

PADLOCK

You are about to unlock a door to success. Your prosperity will surprise you and those who know you.

PAINTING

You will be looking at life in a happier frame of mind. If you enjoy painting, the message is that you have flair.

PALACE

A palace means a good family house move. You may be mixing with wealthy people or visiting a palace.

PALM TREE

Overseas travel will play an important part in your life.

PARCEL

You will receive a very special and particularly pleasing present.

PARROT

A parrot is a portent of gossip which you should avoid spreading.

PEACOCK

Your lifestyle will be one of wealth, and you may become famous.

PEAR

You will have financial success.

PEN

You may need to put pen to paper and might receive a letter or invitation that requires a reply.

PIG

A pig is a sign that you will always have plenty. Perhaps you will visit a farm.

PURSE

You can expect a windfall of money.

PYRAMID

A pyramid is an omen that your spiritual awareness will help you, your family, and your friends.

QUEEN

A woman you are fond of will help you enormously.

QUESTION MARK

You may be wrestling with a problem. But seeing a question mark in the tea leaves is a sure sign that you are soon to find the solution. Before going to sleep, put the problem to the back of your mind. Perhaps the answer will then come to you in your dreams. You will be amazed by how well this works.

It could also mean that somebody who loves you dearly is asking when he or she can show that love to you.

QUEUE

To see a long queue of people reveals that you will learn patience and will come to understand that things usually happen for a good reason.

RABBIT

This lucky emblem heralds that you will overcome shyness and enjoy happy, playful fun, particularly in the spring. Something good could occur at Easter.

To say the phrase *white rabbits* before anything else when you wake up on the first day of a month is believed to ensure that month will be fortunate.

RACKET

This can represent a tennis player. Perhaps you will join a tennis club or go to a tournament. But a racket also means you stand a good chance of winning many of life's battles.

RAILWAY LINE

You may be going on a long and exciting journey. But a railway line also warns that you must not let bad influences make you go off the rails. Your intuition and the bond you have with your parents and family should keep you on the right track.

RAINBOW

A rainbow seen in the morning is a sign that the following day will be wet. To see a rainbow in the afternoon is an omen

that the next day will be fine. But at any time, the appearance of a rainbow is so lucky that you should make a wish.

RATTLE

You will enjoy a happy occasion involving a baby or young children. You may get a babysitting job.

RIDER

You could go horse-riding or win a rosette at a gymkhana.

RING

Someone close will marry. To find out who, look to see if there is an initial near the ring. A number could depict the marriage month. It is also a sign that one day, you too will marry.

RIVER

Everything is flowing your way. You will meet people who lead you towards greater ventures.

ROCKS

An image of rocks in a cup suggests you will overcome a problem by looking at it in a higher frame of mind.

ROSE

A rose reveals that you have a pure heart and that kindness is one of your virtues.

Using a rose, Romany girls charm boys into undying love. Before eating with the boy, they take a sip of spring water without him seeing, dry their lips on the rose and pass it to him during the meal.

RUNNER

If you see someone running you can expect great news to be on its way. You may do well as an athlete or embark on a charity walk.

SACK

A sack denotes a surprise gift.

SADDLE

You may go where there are horses or make a worthwhile journey offering new opportunities.

SCALES

If your birthsign is Libra, you will find your niche in life. The month of your birthday will be especially happy this year. Otherwise, Librans, whose birthdays fall between 24 September and 22 October, may be attracted to you. Mentally, physically, spiritually, and emotionally, everything is balancing in your favor.

SCISSORS

Scissors are a sign that you will speedily accomplish your homework and chores.

SCORPION

This can represent a person born between 23 October and 22 November, under the sign of Scorpio. If it is not your birthsign, someone who is a Scorpio will be helpful to you. When Scorpio is the birthsign for the month you can expect good news and a lucky breakthrough.

SHELL

You will hear pleasing news. You may be invited to go on holiday with a friend's family.

SHIP

You may travel by ship or enjoy a cruise. At the very least, you will go to a place where there are ships.

SHOE

A shoe means you will always be stepping forward in the right direction.

It is believed to be lucky to find a knot in your shoelace. If your right shoelace comes undone, someone is singing your praises. A wish made while tying up someone else's shoelace is likely to come true.

SIGNPOST

The signpost may point to objects which indicate what lies in store. It also means you should read the *signs* people emit, and not necessarily take at face value everything that you see and hear.

SNAKE

Spiritual protection surrounds you if you see a snake. You will grow to be wise.

SPADE

You may have a phase of hard work which later rewards you with success.

SPIDER

The spider, an omen of prosperity and creativity because it spins a web, is a lucky sign. It reveals that you will soon get some new clothes.

Romanies think it is unlucky to kill a spider. They say:

> *If you want to live and thrive,*
> *Let a spider run alive.*

SPOON

You can expect a pleasant surprise if the image of a spoon appears in the tea leaves.

Romanies believe if you accidentally drop a teaspoon, a child will visit.

SQUIRREL

The small things you squirrel away will mount up and become worthwhile.

STAIRS

You are making excellent progress towards a goal; keep persevering.

STAR

Expect a sudden wonderful happening. A star is a symbol of spirit light shining in the darkness. A cluster of small stars reveals that you are very talented. Shooting stars are lucky and should be quickly wished upon before they fade.

Romanies believe that a wish made to the first evening star will come true. They use the country saying:

> *Star light, star bright,*
> *The first star I've seen tonight.*
> *Would it were that I might,*
> *Have the wish I wish tonight.*

STEEPLE

You could achieve a high and mighty aspiration.

SUN

Symbolically, the sun will always shine for you. A holiday and a very happy summer is also forecast.

SWAN

A swan reveals that destiny is at work. An extraordinary and pleasing event is about to happen.

SWING

A swing augurs that you will always remain young at heart. Carefree days lie ahead for you.

TABLE

You will be present at an important discussion or a family reunion.

TEAPOT

Love, fun, and homely happiness are all forecast by a teapot. Not only will you be able to read tea leaves with ease, but also it reveals good news around your mother. You and she will always remain close. You will tell her fortune many times.

Romanies say that stirring tea counterclockwise in a teapot causes a quarrel. If two women pour from the same pot of tea, one of them will have a baby within a year. A teapot lid left open is a sign that a visitor will call.

TELESCOPE

A new era of good fortune is in sight. Keep looking to the future.

TENT

You may be invited on a camping trip.

THISTLE

The special charm of good manners will enable you to deal with *prickly* people.

TOOTHBRUSH

You may soon be packing your toothbrush to stay away from home, or you may be visiting the dentist.

TORCH

You may be the light of someone's life. Is there an initial nearby to tell you who it is?

TORTOISE

Follow your instincts and intuition. Use your sixth sense. You certainly have it.

TREE

A tree seen in your cup indicates that you love the countryside. Numerous trees signify the fulfillment of a wish. If one or several trees are surrounded by dots, your future home could be in the countryside.

TRIANGLE

If you have a heart-felt plan, good fortune and success are certain.

TRUMPET

You may find yourself announcing brilliant news. Without a doubt you will have reason to blow your own trumpet.

TRUNK

A trunk is an omen that life holds great treasures in store for you. A great surprise awaits. Perhaps you will be packing a trunk to travel.

UMBRELLA

Apart from being a sign that you may get caught in the rain, an umbrella shows that you will be protected from harm.

UNICORN

A unicorn reveals that you will succeed where others fail. With concentration, you could soar to great heights.

VASE

You could be receiving or giving flowers.

VIOLIN

You may be involved in a concert. If you play the violin the message is to keep practicing; you could do very well at it.

Some Romany families make a ritual of playing the violin on the night of a full moon. They say it conjures up the spirits of their ancestors.

WAGON

A wagon reveals travel or a change in routine. You may be starting a new school or a new term, or putting a hobby to good use. Somehow, you will get your *show on the road.*

WALKING STICK

A walking stick seen in the leaves means someone you have been longing to see will visit or contact you.

WATERFALL

Good opportunities are flowing your way if a waterfall appears.

WHALE

Your dreams will come true regarding a big wish.

WHEEL

A wheel denotes that the *wheel of fortune* is spinning in your favor. You are on your way up.

WHEELBARROW

Perhaps you will be gardening or discover that you have a flair with plants.

WINDMILL

A windmill shows that you are about to receive approval and help to achieve a desire.

WISHBONE

You will attain your wish.

WITCH

A witch shows that you have magical powers. They will help you to look beyond the obvious, and your insights and intuitions will amaze you.

WOLF

A wolf reveals that you are protected from danger.

YACHT

You may take up sailing. But a holiday or an invitation to spend time with rich friends in opulent surroundings is also forecast by a yacht.

ZEBRA

Sometime in your life you will travel to foreign lands. You may become involved in wildlife organizations.

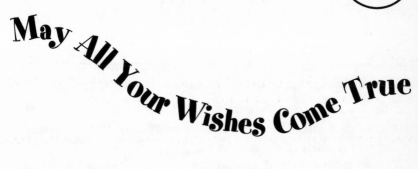

Romany Tea-leaf Wishes
Mutterimengri Chovihoni Booti

When you make a wish it really can come true. The feelings
you put into your wish connect with a power outside yourself in the same way as a prayer does.

When you have made your wish, it is best to keep it a
secret and not to have any doubts about it coming true. If
you expect nothing, you will receive nothing. Negative
thoughts can drag the power back to earth and that will
weaken the energy needed to fulfill your wish. If you
deserve what you have wished for, it will probably be
granted.

Having faith in your wish helps to make it come true.
The Romanies say, *call, and your heart's longings shall*

come to you. Here are some of the secret rituals they used when making wishes.

To Attract Someone

You will need to make your wish on the night of a new moon when the moon appears as a crescent, its curved side on the right and its points to the left. This is the *waxing* moon which means it is growing into a full moon.

❧ Place five teaspoons of tea in an envelope together with a flower to represent the one you desire. You may choose a flower that represents his or her birth sign (see page 81) or one that simply reminds you of your sweetheart. Seal the envelope and place it in a drawer where it should remain undisturbed until the moon is full.

❧ Then make a pot of tea with the tea leaves. After drinking the tea, read your own fortune in the leaves. It should reveal that your sweetheart is attracted to you.

To Strengthen Family Ties

This wish can be used to help stop family squabbles.

❧ Make a pot of tea for your family. Sit together while you pour out a cup for each person and stay until all have finished drinking their tea.

❧ Take a flower pot with a little earth in the bottom and ask all members of the family to place on the soil some of the tea leaves left in their cup.

❧ For each member of the family place one tulip bulb in a circle in the flower pot. You may wish to choose a different colored tulip to represent each person. That way, when the tulips grow you will know which flower represents each parent, brother, or sister. Cover the bulbs with soil.

❧ The roots entwine themselves around each other as they grow, symbolically weaving and strengthening the roots of your family. Your wish grows as the leaves shoot and when the tulips flower, family harmony should flourish.

For A Wish To Come True

❧ Make a pot of tea for your-self. As you do so, place one teaspoon of tea from the packet into an envelope and seal it. As you drink your tea, hold the envelope while making your wish.

❧ Place the envelope in a second envelope which should be put under your pillow and left there for three nights. Go to sleep each night thinking about your wish and asking to dream of it.

❧ After the third night, open the envelopes and scatter the tea leaves under an oak tree, which represents strength. If you do not have an oak tree nearby, find another plant that you feel attracted to and scatter the tea leaves there.

❧ Your wish has now been cast and signs should come that your wish will come true.

To Win His Love

❧ Place five teaspoons of tea in a clean white envelope. Seal the envelope and place it in a drawer beside a photo-graph of yourself.

❧ Invite the one you desire to have a cup of tea with you.

❧ When he arrives, make a pot of tea from the contents of the envelope and drink the tea together. Read his tea leaves for him.

❧ When your beloved has gone, empty the leaves from his cup under a rose bush because roses represent love. As the rose grows, so will his affection for you.

❧ If you do not have a rose bush, empty his tea leaves into a flower pot partially filled with earth. On top of it, plant a hyacinth bulb to represent fun, then surround the bulb with soil. Your sweetheart's love for you should grow and flourish, especially when the hyacinth blooms.

To Get Him to Contact You

❧ Make a pot of tea. Light a candle and pour yourself a cup of tea.

❧ When you have finished drinking, lift the cup into the air and swirl the tea leaves around the cup three times in a large counterclockwise circle before placing it upside down on the saucer.

❧ Gaze into the cup until you have drifted into a dreamy state of mind, imagining the figures in the cup living in the way you want them to. In your mind, tell the person you are thinking of to get in touch with you by telephone or letter, or by calling at your home, or to be where you are likely to meet him. Desiring something with all your heart will help you to establish a connection with it. And believing that you will get your wish will help to make it come true. Be sure to wish only for good things. Romanies say the good you think or do will come back to you ten-fold.

❧ Write your sweetheart's name on a small piece of paper. Burn it in a candle flame and place it on a saucer to extinguish itself. Snuff out the candle. You will soon get the one you want.

CHAPTER 4

Say It With Flowers

The Romany Language of Flowers
Rosalo-jib

As well as being fragrant and beautiful, flowers have always had great symbolic importance for us.

Lucky *white heather* has always been associated with the Romanies. Hawking it from door to door, Gypsy women used to try selling it to the *gorgios*, the non-Gypsy house-dwellers, by saying, "Buy some lucky heather. Cross my palm with silver, dearie, and you'll be blessed."

In recent years when conservation rights prohibited the picking of certain wild flowers in Britain, the resourceful Romanies resorted to making crepe-paper flowers to sell instead. Seated around the campfire, the men also made chrysanthemum flowers from elder wood which they shaved with a penknife.

When the seasons offered a variety of wild flowers the women would sell posies. These were sometimes composed of certain flowers each of which possessed a meaning that helped to work a specific wish. Most people today know one red rose means *I love you*. But other flowers have symbolic meanings, too. The Romanies used flowers, herbs, fruit, and grass in their secret language which they called *rosalo-jib*.

Romanies managed their lives without clocks and calendars. They told the time by noticing how dark or light the sky was. They knew it was midday when the sun was at its highest in the heavens. They marked the passing seasons by their knowledge of plants and trees and by the behavior of wild animals and birds.

Romanies are particularly fond of two wild plants. One is called *traveler's joy*, which most people know as *wild clematis* or *old man's beard*. Scrambling among hedgerows, its white and green flowers that bloom in May and June are a traveler's companions. When summer fades the flowers become wispy white seedheads which are blown away by the wind. Romany girls pick a seedhead and ask, "Does he love me?" She then blows the seeds away and with each puff of breath she says alternately, "Yes," and "No," until the last puff reveals the answer.

The other wild plant beloved by the Romanies is the *prickly lettuce* which acts as a compass. The leaves, which are spiky underneath, twist in sunlight to point north and south. Looking at the sun and the direction in which the leaves are growing indicates to the Romanies which direction to take.

Some flowers and herbs represent the hours of a clock. The Romanies could arrange to meet one another at a certain place and time by conveying a secret message in a posy of flowers and herbs.

When a courting Gypsy couple were chaperoned by a third person, they could pass one another a secret message using flowers and herbs to say what words could not convey. The posy a boy gave to his sweetheart spoke volumes to her.

A Romany Floral Clock

Each hour of the day is represented by a flower or herb.

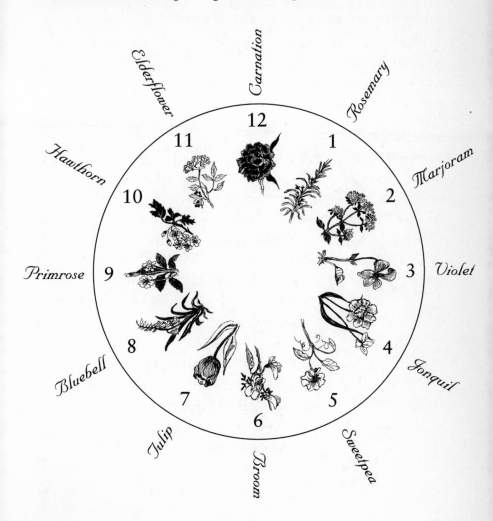

A Romany Floral Calendar

The months of the year are each represented by a flower.

January ❧ Snowdrops

February ❧ Crocus and primroses

March ❧ Daffodils and violets

April ❧ Daisies

May ❧ Lilies of the valley, hawthorn, and cowslips

June ❧ Roses and honeysuckle

July ❧ Carnations

August ❧ Gladioli and poppies

September ❧ Michaelmas daisies

October ❧ Dahlias and goldenrod

November ❧ Chrysanthemums

December ❧ Holly

A Romany Zodiac

 ARIES ★ 21 March–20 April

Anemones, daffodils, crowsfoot, cuckoopint, mustard, chives, garlic, and basil – all ruled by the planet Mars.

 TAURUS ★ 21 April–20 May

White lily, burdock, golden-rod, clover, lovage, peppermint, heather, laurel, and primroses – all ruled by the planet Venus.

 GEMINI ★ 21 May–21 June

Clover, lavender, meadowsweet, valerian, mulberry, and parsley – all ruled by the planet Mercury.

 CANCER ★ 22 June–23 July

Honeysuckle, rosemary, mistletoe, wild rose, and lemon balm – all ruled by the Moon.

 LEO ★ 24 July–23 August

Marigolds, St John's Wort, bay, sorrel, great celandine, and chamomile – all ruled by the Sun.

VIRGO ★ 24 August–23 September

Oregano, azalea, tansy, dill, marjoram, lily of the valley, and vervain – all ruled by Mercury.

LIBRA ★ 24 September–22 October

Thyme, apple blossom, columbines, cowslips, roses, and burdock – all ruled by Venus.

SCORPIO ★ 23 October–22 November

Orchids, poppies, heather, bramble, wormwood, and blackthorn – all ruled by Pluto.

SAGITTARIUS ★ 23 November–22 December

Dandelion, houseleek, chicory, chervil, dock, oak, sage, and agrimony – all ruled by Jupiter.

CAPRICORN ★ 23 December–20 January

Ivy, Christmas rose, Solomon's seal, henbane, comfrey – all ruled by Saturn.

AQUARIUS ★ 21 January–19 February

Quince, comfrey, campion, monkshood, gladioli, and holly – all ruled by Saturn.

PISCES ★ 20 February–20 March

Burnet, verbain, woodruff – all ruled by Neptune.

Basic Rules of *Rosalo-jib*

Before a message given in flowers and herbs can be understood, both the giver and the receiver need to know the ground rules. Even then, there can be confusing mix-ups and mistakes over the time, date, and place of a meeting. And, of course, unless paper or carved flowers were used, a message given in flowers or herbs had to be made up of whatever plants were available.

❦ Romanies consider it good luck both to give and to receive flowers. They say it is luckier to give an odd number of flowers than an even number.

❦ It is said to be unlucky to pick up a flower seen lying in the road. To do so is to pick up sorrow.

❦ Romanies think it is unlucky to bring into their *vardos* (caravans) any flowers that have bloomed out of season.

❦ Red flowers are thought to give strength, and are particularly appropriate if given to a person who is ill. Romanies believe the color red represents blood. It is unlucky to give or receive red and white flowers together because they represent blood and bandages. Pink flowers are said to be the color of love.

❦ Romanies say that purple flowers attract money and that yellow flowers radiate warmth and invite good fortune. To wish for wealth when you come across the first spring daffodil in bloom

is a sure sign that the year will bring more gold than silver.

🍃 It is very lucky to catch a falling leaf. Romanies say it ensures you will have 12 months of happiness. Leaves that blow into a caravan or house are also a sign of good luck.

🍃 Romanies say you should be wary of anyone who cannot hold a flower without it wilting or dropping its petals. They believe the flower is detecting unkindness in the person.

🍃 A flower given upright carries a positive message. One red rose means *I love you.*

🍃 A flower given upside-down gives the negative message, *I do not love you.*

🍃 Persons wanting to talk about their own feelings should lean a flower to the left as they pass it to a friend. A clear message could be conveyed with a sprig of *forget-me-nots.*

🍃 To comment to a friend about his or her feelings, lean the flower to the right as you hand it to him or her. To give lavender in this way clearly says, *I know you love me.*

🍃 The answer to a question is *yes* if a flower is returned with the right hand and *no* if it is passed back with the left hand.

🍃 Where the knot is tied in the ribbon round a posy also says something. If, when facing the posy, the knot is to the left it explains something about the giver. If the knot is on the right it asks a question or makes a statement.

❧ If you are given a flower and you wear it leaning to your right it says that you understand the feelings of the person who has given it to you. Leaning to the left, the flower expresses the emotion you feel for that person. If a Romany girl wore a flower in her hair it warned her boyfriend to be discreet. If she wore it on her heart, she was openly declaring her love.

Talking with Flowers

Romanies; who are superstitious by nature, hold flowers and herbs in high esteem. They can predict the weather and carry secret messages. A gift of flowers brings joy as their color and fragrance lift a person's spirits. Herbs also give additional comfort and are used by Romanies for healing as well as in cooking. Every plant, whether it is an enormous tree or a tiny weed, is unique. And so is every single part of it – each flower, leaf, fruit, or herb. For that reason alone, they are quite magical.

Following are some of the meanings that are understood by Romanies whenever they give or receive flowers.

Rosalo-jib
The Romany Language of Flowers

ANEMONE: *Fleeting love.*

Anemones, which appear in early spring, easily lose their petals if a chilly wind blows. This is why they mean *love may be short-lived.*

APPLE BLOSSOM: *Temptation.*

Apple blossom, ruled by the love planet, Venus, acquired the reputation of temptation because Eve gave Adam an apple to eat in the Garden of Eden.

Romanies say apple blossom should not be brought into a caravan or house because, when indoors, it is a sign of ill health.

When apples are abundant on the branches, Romanies say it is an omen that a lot of twins will be born within 12 months.

To see the sun shining through the branches of an apple tree on Christmas day is a sure sign of a good harvest of apples in the New Year. It is an omen of a bad crop if an apple remains on a branch throughout the winter.

What is My True Love's Name?

Romany girls play a game to find the initial of a future boyfriend. They call out a letter of the alphabet each time they twist the stalk of an apple. The letter spoken as the stalk breaks will be the initial of his name.

❧ ♥ ❧

Another way to divine a future boyfriend is to slice an apple into nine segments. Stand in front of a mirror lit only by candlelight. One by one, hold up above the left shoulder each of the segments on the point of the knife. His image, Romanies say, will be reflected in the mirror.

ASTER: *Second thoughts.*

A variety of the Michaelmas daisy, asters are used by Romanies to predict whether they will have success in a business deal. Alternately saying, *I shall* and *I shall not* with each petal plucked will reveal the answer as the last one goes.

BACHELOR'S BUTTON: *Faithfulness.*

A Romany girl takes the yellow flower from her sweetheart's buttonhole to test whether he truly loves her. If it fades in her pocket overnight, so will his love for her.

BAY: *Eternal love.*

Because bay, or laurel as it is also called, is an evergreen, it represents undying love and affection. Ruled by the Sun and the birth sign Leo, it is particularly suitable to give to a Leo. Bay is a sign of victory. The crowning of poets with laurel symbolized triumph over inner conflict.

Romanies, who say the tree is sacred to Apollo, the god of love and light, hang bunches of bay leaves in their caravans to enhance romance. They also use bay leaves to divine what will happen in the future.

To find out whether her sweetheart loves her, a Romany girl will scratch a cross on a bay leaf before slipping it into her shoe and wearing it all day long. On going to bed she will leave the leaf in her shoe. The following morning, if the cross has turned brown, it is a sign that he loves her.

Sitting at the campfire with a handful of bay leaves, Romanies ask a *yes* or *no* question. Then they throw the bay leaves into the flames. If the leaves crackle and burn noisily, the answer is *yes*. If they burn silently, the answer is *no*.

Romany lovers who wish to stay in love pick a twig from

a bay tree. The girl snaps the twig in half so that she and her partner can each keep a piece.

BINDWEED: *Modesty.*

This common pink or white wild flower entwines itself around other plants and crawls along grass verges. It is thought to be humble because it needs other plants for survival.

BLUEBELL: *Constancy, I am true.*

The wild hyacinth that flowers in April and May is believed to have healing powers. Sitting in a bluebell wood is said to calm the mind because blue is regarded as a healing color.

BRAMBLE: *Virginal purity.*

The pink flowers that grow on the blackberry bush are ruled by the love planet Venus and the birth sign Aries.

To alleviate illness Romanies place nine bramble leaves in a bowl of spring water. One by one the leaves are then passed over the afflicted person. Afterwards the leaves are burned or buried in the belief that as they perish so will the illness.

On their wedding night, Romany girls place bramble flowers under their pillows as an emblem of virginal purity consumed by the flame of passion.

BROOM: *Ardor.*

Broom's bright yellow flowers, which bloom in April, May, and June, are believed to express the warm feeling of love.

In the belief that it will bring them luck, Romanies sometimes wear sprigs of broom flowers and carry seed pods of broom.

But they say it is unlucky to bring broom indoors in May because it is a sign that one of the family will go away.

BUTTERCUP: *Happiness.*

Romanies say it is a promise of riches if a buttercup or kingcup reflects a bright gold color on a person's face or neck when the flower is held up close to them.

CARNATION: *Pure love.*

Carnations, popularly pinned in the buttonholes of guests at weddings, are worn to symbolize the love of the couple getting married.

CHRISTMAS TREE: *Eternal life.*

Romanies believe that the evergreen Christmas tree provides winter refuge for woodland spirits until other trees regain their leaves. A decorated Christmas tree, indoors or out, enhances the spirit of Christmas by bringing a feeling of well-being.

CHRYSANTHEMUM

Red ✌ *I love you.*
Yellow ✌ *You have upset me.*
White ✌ *Honesty.*
The name *chrysanthemum* is sometimes shortened to *'mum*. They are perfect flowers to give to mothers, especially on Mother's Day.

CLOVER: *Happiness.*

An emblem of the Holy Trinity, these simple flowers grow in lawns and are full of nectar which attracts honey bees, making both bees and humans contented.

CROCUS: *Youthful happiness.*

These flowers announce the arrival of spring, but soon depart, like childhood.

Romanies say, if you see a crocus in bloom on St Valentine's Day, February 14, you will be lucky in love for the remainder of the year.

DAFFODIL: *Chivalry.*
Good manners.

Daffodils are considered to be well mannered because they usually allow crocus to make their debut first.

DAHLIA: *Insecurity*.

Dahlias originated in Mexico. It took many years of greenhouse nurturing before they became hardy enough to endure our colder climates. This is why they are vulnerable.

DAISY: *Innocence*.

The daisy is ruled by the planet Venus and the birth sign Cancer. Its familiar name among Romanies is *day's eye* because it opens in sunshine and closes at dusk. Pulling the petals out of a daisy head one by one while reciting *he loves me, he loves me not* will, by the last petal plucked, reveal whether a girl's boyfriend is in love with her.

Romanies say a daisy chain means *I respond to your love, but give me time to think about it.* The circular chain represents the sun which sustains the earth. Wearing a daisy chain is believed to protect a person from harm.

DANDELION: *Oracle*.

The humble dandelion predicts the weather by opening its flowers in sunshine and closing them when it's about to rain or get dark.

The seed heads are also said to act as clocks by telling the time according to the number of puffs of breath needed to rid it of its silky down. A single blow represents one o'clock, two blows two o'clock, and so on.

The number of puffs it takes to blow away the seed

heads of a dandelion can also tell a girl how many years she will wait before marrying.

A dandelion seed head can tell a girl who is separated from her lover whether or not he is faithful. Thinking of him she picks the seed head and holds it up to face north, south, east, or west, according to the direction he is in. Thinking of him, she blows the fluffy down to send him a message. If one or more seeds remain attached after a second puff, then he is true.

ELDER: *Guardian.*

A symbol of protection, elder flowers arrive in summer and depart leaving purple berries. Romanies call elder, which is ruled by Venus, the *witch tree.* As an amulet to keep harm away, some carry walking sticks carved from elder, a tree of magic. Others carry an elder twig with several knots in it as a strong protective charm.

Because the mother of all elves, the Elder Queen, is said to live in its roots, Romanies will not cut elder trees without first asking the tree's permission. Nor will they burn elder on their fires because it would invite misfortune.

In the past, Romanies have made elder *candles* by cutting the pith of branches into flat round shapes. These were dipped into oil and lit floating in a bowl of water.

EVERLASTING: *Everlasting love.*

Because everlasting flowers dry rather than die, they mean *I will always love you.*

As a gesture of enduring affection, Romanies place everlasting in wedding bouquets and also on graves.

EVENING PRIMROSE: *Romantic nights.*

The evening primrose which unfolds at dusk comes out to play when other flowers are retiring for the night.

FORGET-ME-NOT: *Love me. Do not forget me.*

The simple meaning of the tiny blue forget-me-not is that persons in love cannot forget the ones loved. Their lovers are constantly in their thoughts.

FOXGLOVE: *Pride.*

Romanies also call it *witch's thimble* and *fairy flower.*

GERANIUM: *Comfort.*

Romanies say the scent of a geranium is rather like a smelling salt which brings comfort.

GLADIOLI: *Good news.*

Ruled by Saturn, which symbolizes time, gladioli mean good news and happy activities.

HAREBELL: *Grief.*

Because this delicate blue flower droops its head it appears sad.

HAWTHORN: *Faith.*

Happiness and future hopes are symbolized by hawthorn. May, as it is also known, should not be brought inside because it is an omen that someone in the home will become ill.

But outdoors, Romanies use it as a protective charm against misfortune. They sometimes offer branches to newlyweds and place boughs by new-born babies.

HELLEBORE: *Purity.*

This small white flower is commonly known as the Christmas rose. Romanies believe that this first grew in the gardens

of heaven and was looked after by the angels who called it the rose of love. When the winter snow came to Eden and not one flower remained, the angels asked God to let them carry this one flower to earth as a token of his love.

HOLLY: *Happiness.*

Known as the *holy tree* since medieval times, Romanies credit holly with the power to ward off evil spirits. Some Gypsies refer to Holly as *Christ's thorn* because the prickly leaves and scarlet berries represent Christ's suffering.

To dream who will be their future lover, Romany girls hold a handkerchief as they pick nine smooth-edged holly leaves on a Friday evening. They then tie nine knots in the handkerchief and place it under their pillow.

At Christmas, Romanies make holly wreaths to sell. Because the smooth leaves are said to be female and the prickly leaves male, both types must be woven together to create harmony. If only the prickly leaves are used, the man will dominate the home and if only smooth leaves are used, the woman will rule the roost.

No Romany would ever destroy a holly tree. To do so is an act of blasphemy that would invite disaster to him and his family.

HONEYSUCKLE: *Fidelity.*

Honeysuckle faithfully clings to whatever it has entwined itself around.

HYACINTH: *Fun.*

The hyacinth is traditionally used in
Romany bridal crowns and wreaths for its
sweet fragrance and light-hearted message
of happiness.

The crown is symbolic of a *queen*. Sometimes,
Romany men would wear a *king's* crown of
foliage to represent the harmonious union of
the conscious and unconscious, the perfect
marriage of husband and wife, heaven and
earth, sun and moon, and gold and silver.

HYDRANGEA: *I will not marry you.*

Romanies say a hydrangea growing
close to a person's front door is a sign
that a daughter in the house will not
marry.

IRIS: *I have good news for you.*

Iris, which can bloom in a variety of colors,
derived its name from Iris, a messenger who is
the goddess of the rainbow.

A wish should be made when a rainbow

appears, because the rainbow is believed to be a living spirit which carries the wish to heaven.

IVY: *I will cling to you.*

Ivy's evergreen leathery leaves and yellow flowers are often placed in the wedding bouquets of Romanies and non-Romanies as a sign of fidelity and marriage.

But because ivy sometimes strangles the trees and plants it clings to and visibly makes some flowers wilt when placed in the same vase, it can also be regarded as bad.

On Hallowe'en, October 31, Romany girls divine using ivy leaves. Each girl picks an ivy leaf, scores it with an individual mark, such as a cross, and passes it through a gold earring. The leaves are then placed in a bowl of water. The following morning, if black spots have appeared on the ivy it is sign of romance with a dark-haired man. If black spots virtually cover the leaf, the girl will marry a dark-haired man within a year. If no spots emerge, no special lover will arrive within the next 12 months.

JASMINE: *Attraction.*

Jasmine which releases its sweet, strong fragrance on summer evenings is picked and placed in Romany caravans to enhance romance.

LAVENDER: *Acknowledgement of love.*

Lavender is ruled by the planet Mercury which governs mental and physical communication. Romanies place lavender stems in their caravans to scent the air. They also place it under their pillows for a peaceful night's sleep as well as in drawers to keep moths away.

LILAC: *Love's first emotions.*

Romanies say it is unlucky to take lilac, which they call *fairy ladders,* indoors. To find a lilac blossom with eight petals is an omen of love.

LILY

White ☙ *purity.*
Yellow ☙ *enchantment.*
For centuries, white lilies have been depicted in the stained-glass windows and carved stone of churches because they represent innocence and purity and are symbolic of good over evil. Today, they are still carried to church in wedding bouquets and funeral wreaths.

Romanies believe that it is unlucky to break or tread on a lily. To do so is a sign that a girl or woman in their midst will innocently come to harm.

LILY OF THE VALLEY: *Return of happiness.*

Lily of the valley, which appears in May, is ruled by the fast-moving planet Mercury. Romanies say the nightingale bird would not return to the wood until the flower bloomed each spring.

To wish each other a happy month, Romanies traditionally give each other a lily of the valley flower on the first day of May, which is known as May Day.

May is an important month in which many Romanies worship their patron saint, St. Sara of Egypt. Since 1450 Romanies from all over the world have gathered on May 24 at the shrine of St. Sara of Egypt. Medallions of the sick are pressed against the statue, and scarves and rags are hung around it in the crypt of the church of Les Saintes Maries de la Mer in the Camargue region of France.

On May 25, to represent the original migration of Gypsies overseas, the statue of St. Sara the black virgin is carried by a procession into the sea and then returned to the crypt. The profound factor of this Gypsy meeting is that no matter what country the Romanies have traveled from to visit the Catholic church, they all speak Romanes.

LUPIN: *Sadness.*

The lupin appears melancholy and lonely because at sunset, it folds its drooping leaves around itself as if for comfort.

MARIGOLD: *A wealthy marriage.*

Marigolds are also called calendula because there is at least one variety in flower during every month of the year.

The orange flower, which opens its petals at dawn and closes them at dusk, is ruled by the sun and the star sign Leo. Romany girls wear marigold flowers to increase their chances of attracting a wealthy partner.

MINT: *Warmth.*

Romanies say that if mint flourishes in your garden, you are sure to be wealthy.

MIMOSA: *Sensitivity.*

Romanies call it the *sensitive plant* because it shrinks from even the lightest fingertip touch and has the same shy reaction when clouds appear.

MISTLETOE: *Family happiness.*

Mistletoe, a mystical parasitic plant that grows on oak trees, has been regarded as so sacred by some Romanies that it could only be cut with a golden sickle in December.

They gather it to sell and hang in their caravans as a sign to restore and regenerate family life.

When mistletoe withers and the branch turns yellow, Romanies believe it has the power to guide them to buried treasure.

At Christmas, the tradition of kissing under the mistletoe lives on. Romanies believe a berry should be removed with each kiss.

NARCISSUS: *Unrequited love.*

Narcissus takes its name from a Greek myth. Narcissus was a vain, handsome youth who rejected the love of an admirer, Echo. So angry were the gods, they condemned him to lose his heart to his own image in a pool of water. Day and night he gazed at his reflection until he pined away and died. In pity the gods changed him into a flower bearing his name.

NASTURTIUM: *Passion.*

These red, orange, and yellow flowers are hot in color and taste. The leaves taste similar to watercress and can be eaten in salads.

OAK: *Strength.*

Sacred to Jupiter, the planet of money, luck, and travel, oak trees are worshiped by some Romanies. Those that have mistletoe growing from their branches are thought to be especially powerful. Like all trees, oaks represent a world axis because their branches in the sky and roots in the soil link heaven and earth.

In fine weather, Romanies who feel depleted in energy ask the oak if they may stand barefoot beside the tree-trunk to receive its strong, healing powers.

ORCHID: *Perfect lover.*

Also called *lady's slipper*, an orchid represents feminine charm. Ruled by Venus, orchids attract love.

In tropical forests orchids grow hanging from trees in bright splashes of color, appearing unreal in a lonely and dangerous world.

For millionaire enthusiasts, orchid hunters in the nineteenth century faced death searching for orchids in the jungle. Not all orchids grow on trees. Today, there are more than a thousand varieties, making orchids easier to find than the perfect lover!

PANSY: *Thought.*

Also called *heart's-ease*, pansy means *loving, tender thoughts*. Because the planet Saturn, which represents restriction and limitation, rules the pansy the flower also means loving from a distance. Some Romanies say it means *think of me while we are parted.*

PASSIONFLOWER: *Religious beliefs.*

The passionflower is said to represent Christ's crucifixion. The crown above the petals is the crown of thorns. The five stamens are five wounds, and the three styles are nails. The ten sepals and petals symbolize the ten disciples who remained faithful. Friends who witnessed Jesus being nailed to the cross stand in the outer corona.

PEONY: *Protection.*

In the belief that it will help their teeth to grow, young Romany children wear necklaces of beads fashioned from peony roots.

PERIWINKLE: *Instant attraction.*

The bright blue periwinkle, which appears in March and April, is ruled by the love planet Venus. A Romany boy who wanted to find a sweetheart would place one in his buttonhole as a sign that he was available.

PINKS: *Romantic lover.*

Pinks, feminine, frilly flowers, *pretty pinks* and *maiden pinks* as the Romanies call them, flower in May and June, exuding a carnation-like scent.

Since pink is the color of love, flesh, sensuality, and emotions, Romany girls place pinks under their pillows in the hope that they will bring them dreams of their perfect lover.

POINSETTIA: *Heaven blessed.*

Romanies call poinsettia the *flower of the holy night*. Its flaming star of scarlet leaves, which appears at Christmas, is likened to the star of Bethlehem. Poinsettias often feature on Christmas cards and are given as yule gifts.

POPPY: *Grief.*

Red poppies, which Romanies call *corn-roses*, appear in corn fields in July and August. As well as the scarlet field poppy, there are white, pink, rose, yellow, and orange varieties. Their flaming beauty, which creates a riot of color, is to summer what the tulip is to spring.

Romanies say a poppy petal held in the left palm and hit with the right fist should make a *popping* sound if your sweetheart is faithful.

PRIMROSE: *Young love.*

The primrose, which appears in early spring, inspires hope because the year is young enough to attract romance.

REED: *Music.*

Reeds often grow close to water which makes music with its ripples as they dance downstream. But reed also relates to Pan the pipe playing god of universal nature who stood for all Greek gods and the old religion, paganism.

Among the Welsh Gypsies, some marrying couples made a ring from rushes until they could afford a gold one. All rings are symbolic of continuity and wholeness. Other marrying couples plucked hairs from their heads and plaited them to make a ring. A ring is a symbol of marriage and also of the perpetual and repeated cycle of time in the universe.

Many Romany men worked as scrap-metal merchants. A spin-off was that they made their own sovereign rings and wedding bands by melting broken gold and silver spoons, brooches, buckles, and coins.

Gypsy girls foretell their own marriage prospects using a borrowed wedding ring. Over a glass of water taken from a south-flowing stream the girl suspends a ring tied to a hair from her own head. If the ring swings in a circle around the rim, marriage is certain. If it hits the rim, she will not marry the one she has in mind.

ROSE

Red ⁊❧ *I love you.*
Red rosebud ⁊❧ *You are beautiful.*
Pink ⁊❧ *Everlasting love.*
Golden ⁊❧ *Achievement.*
Yellow ⁊❧ *Jealousy.*
White ⁊❧ *Secrecy.*
Ruled by the love planet Venus, the rose more than any other flower represents love and ardor's emotional pleasure and pain. Wild roses have heart-shaped petals. Rose's exotic fragrance and beautiful petals represent the happiness of love. Its thorns are love's painful feelings. People seek and find one another, part and hurt each other.

The essence in a single rose is a symbol of completion,

achievement, perfection. It represents the heart and the mystic center.

The blue rose is symbolic of the unachievable, while the golden rose is symbolic of absolute achievement. A rose with eight petals symbolizes regeneration. One with seven petals relates to the seven planets and seven days of the week.

Worldwide, the rose is treasured as a sacred flower because of its scent and beauty. The word *rosary* is derived from the Latin for rose garden. Churches use the red rose to symbolize Christ's blood and the white rose as a symbol of the Virgin Mary's purity.

The Tudor rose, the floral emblem of England, has an inner row of red petals and an outer row of white. When Henry VII (1457-1509) married Princess Elizabeth of York, he united his red rose of Lancaster badge with her white rose of York emblem.

On midsummer night's eve, June 20, Romany girls pick a rosebud, fold it in a piece of paper and leave it undisturbed until Christmas Day. On that day they wear it in the belief that they will attract their future partner. If the rosebud has turned brown, the charm will be useless that day.

Romanies say the heart of a roaming lover may be won on midsummer night's eve by picking three roses. At midnight, one must be buried under a yew tree and another at a church gate. The third rose must be placed under the girl's pillow and left there for three nights. The following day, she must burn this last rose, after which her lover will dream of her constantly until he is compelled to return.

If petals fall from a rose while a person is holding the

stem in their hand, it is a sign of illness. The antidote is for the person to snap a fallen petal between the fingers. Romany girls also break a fallen petal with their fingers to determine whether they are loved. A loud noise reveals an admirer's passion is strong.

Romanies also say that planting an onion beside a rose enhances the rose's sweet smell and that garlic planted in a rosebed deters bugs from eating the rose.

To heal a heart broken by love, Romany girls scatter rose petals in a river or stream. The pain ebbs away when the current takes the petals downstream.

ROSEMARY: *Remembrance.*

It is customary for Rosemary to be woven into bridal bouquets as a symbol of fidelity in love. Wedding guests carry a sprig or two of rosemary in their pockets to bring success in love, to wish the couple good luck, to keep harm away, and to help the whole congregation to remember the wedding day. A sprig of rosemary is often slipped into floral arrangements for luck.

At funerals, mourners carry a sprig to throw on to the coffin after it has been lowered into the ground. They believe it helps the spirit to rest, knowing they will not be forgotten by those they have left behind.

On other occasions, Gypsies wear rosemary sprigs for success in love and work. Because they believe it improves the memory, they cook a sprig or two in stews. They also drink tissanes of rosemary by steeping a few sprigs in a teapot of boiling water. Any of the *tea* left over in the pot is used for rinsing their hair to darken and strengthen it.

ROWAN: *Protection. I will look after you.*

In the belief that it keeps harm away, Gypsies hang rowan berries in tiny cloth bags around the necks of their babies. Romanies say that finding a rowan leaf with an equal number of small leaflets is very lucky and it should be carried with you always.

Welsh Gypsies used to carve shepherd's crooks from rowan roots. The crooks were believed to ward off bad spirits. The tree, sometimes called mountain ash, was also used to cut into hoops to strengthen barrels, and for making black dye. By reciting a rhyme, Romanies divine spring weather with rowan.

> *If the ash is out before the oak,*
> *Then we're going to have a soak.*
> *But if the oak's before the ash,*
> *Then we'll only get a splash.*

SAGE: *Wisdom.*

Ruled by Jupiter, which governs mental and physical development, sage is said to grow especially well for those who are wise. Eating small amounts of the herb is believed by

Romanies to strengthen their mind and memory as well as increase their chances of a long life. They regard it is a lucky plant.

When a family member goes away, Romanies sometimes hang a sage sprig in their caravans for divination. It is a sign the absent person is well if the sprig does not wilt.

At midnight on midsummer night's eve, Romany girls pick 12 sage leaves. They hold the sage and look over their shoulder, hoping to see their future partner either in person or in their imagination.

SNOWDROP: *Hope.*

Romanies call the snowdrop the *fair maid of February*, and also *the morning star of flowers*. It means fresh starts, consolation, and comfort. But because of its shroud-like appearance, the delicate white flower is thought to be an omen of death if brought indoors.

SUNFLOWER: *Brightness.*

Symbolic of the Sun, the golden sunflower means bright and happy days. Romanies say sunflowers attract wealth when planted in a garden.

STRAWBERRY BLOSSOM:
Perfection.

Delicate white strawberry flowers represent perfect friendship. Romany children make a wish when they eat their first strawberry of the year.

THYME: *Activity.*

Thyme, ruled by Venus, has a scent that restores energy and attracts busy bees. According to Romanies, it also entices fairies, who are said to dance around thyme on Midsummer Night's Eve, June 20th.

On that night, Romany girls steep a few thyme sprigs in boiling water. They drink the hot brew and make a wish for the one they desire.

Romanies believe almost anyone can see fairies dancing around a candle if they stare at the flame until compelled to close their eyes. When they open their eyes again and look at the flame, fairies will be visible.

Fairies do humble tasks for people, flowers, and all nature. Not only do they bless new-born babies with gifts of wisdom, they can also conjure people, palaces, and miracles to appear in people's lives.

But for fairy magic to work, a person must first believe in fairies.

TULIP: *Love*

There is nothing timid about tulips which are unequaled in color and variety by any other flower.

Tulip bulbs were introduced to Europe from Turkey. In 1634, *tulip mania* became rampant in Holland which was the hub of bulb production. There, tulip bulbs were sold by the weight like diamonds. The craze lasted for four years.

VIOLET: *Faithfulness.*

Romanies sometimes sell small bunches of tiny violets which flower in March. They represent faithfulness because the flowers are said to be at one with heaven and earth.

WALLFLOWER: *Faithfulness in sadness.*

Before the wallflower was cultivated, the strongly scented flower seeded itself in the walls of castle ruins where little else flourished.

WHITE HEATHER: *Pure good luck.*

White heather is the lucky flower of the Romanies. White is feminine and holy.

Colorful Revelations

Pure emotions such as love, sadness, loss, fear, anger, and jealousy are all represented by the three *primary* colors, red, yellow, and blue.

Because very young children experience pure emotions rather than mixed feelings, they usually pick primary color flowers because they relate to them better.

Adults have more complex feelings so, subconsciously, they are attracted to yellowish mauve, near violet, and green-ish-yellow flowers. These are *secondary* colors, created by mixing the three primary colors. Children and pure thinkers are less likely to choose flowers that are secondary colors.

The seven colors of the rainbow, red, yellow, orange, blue, green, indigo, and violet, represent the seven colors of the soul. They also signify seven positive virtues, seven vices, seven days of the week, and seven planets.

Your character is revealed not only by the color of the flowers you prefer but also by the colors you choose in every aspect of your life. This includes the colors you choose to wear and those you like to have around you in your environment. Romanies who tell fortunes use their observation of a person's color choices to gain insight about the character of the person.

Color preferences speak volumes about personality and situations, probably without a person being aware of it. Color preferences can change from day to day according to how a person feels or what mood they are in.

As you begin to read fortunes, let a person's color preferences influence what you have to say about them. Here is what the Romanies understand colors to mean.

RED: *Passion*

The life-giving principle, pulsing blood, and fire, aggressive emotions, passion, sentiment, and power are all indicated by the color red.

YELLOW: *Intuition*

Yellow represents sunlight, and Apollo the ancient Greek god of light, poetry, music, healing, and prophecy. Yellow is the far-seeing sun, shining rays of light in darkness. When sunlight disappears again into the darkness of nightfall, it illuminates intuition and reveals remarkable future happenings and intellect.

BLUE: *True thought*

Blue is the color of the air's rarified atmosphere and the deep blue sea. It represents spiritual thoughts and the soul within the body.

Secondary Colors

ORANGE: *Ambition*

Orange, a combination of red and yellow, represents fire, flames, and emotional pride.

GREEN: *Sympathy*

Green, produced by mixing blue for thoughts and yellow for intuition, creates the earthly color of living plants and trees. Green is the sensation of nature ruled by the love goddess, Venus.

VIOLET: *Spirituality and nostalgia*

Power and spirituality are represented by violet which is made by mixing red for passion and blue for devotion. Memories are created because violet combines red and blue.

Tertiary Colors

Tertiary colors are made by combining secondary colors. They are dark and represent subtle emotions that are hard to define. The shades of color are feelings and reactions working at the deepest levels of a person's psyche.

Other Colors

INDIGO: *Intuitive spiritual thoughts*

Indigo is a mixture of the secondary color violet, for spirituality, and the primary color blue, for true thoughts. It represents ideas inspired by omnipotence (a state of all-knowing).

PINK: *Emotions*

Pink, a light version of red, relates to flesh. It links the sensuality of the body with the emotions of the mind.

GOLD: *Glory*

Gold is divine light. The mystic aspect of the sun is represented by gold. In Latin, the word for gold is *aurum* which sounds rather like aura. In Hebrew it means light. Gold represents the superior part of every person, the fruits of the spirit. By its millions of journeys around the earth it is as if the sun has spun golden threads around the world.

SILVER: *Mystic thoughts*

Silver represents the mystic, reflective aspect of the moon.

BLACK: *Time*

Germination in darkness, fertilized land, and mineral life are all represented by black. Carbon is black in coal but sparklingly clear when crystalized in a diamond.

WHITE: *Tireless ecstasy*

Intuition, illumination, revelation, and sacred forgiveness are expressed by white, a shining light of the supernatural.

Amaze Your Friends

You are now ready to read fortunes using the language of flowers. Here's what you do.

❊ Invite your friends around. Ask them all to bring with them one flower that they really like. You must not see what flower each person has brought, so arrange for your friends to place their flowers on a tray or a table out of your sight.

❊ With your friends around you, pick up one of the flowers and hold it. Knowing what the flower means and what its color symbolizes will suggest to you how your friend feels. You may be able to read the thoughts of the person who brought the flower, whether or not that friend realizes the significance of their choice. Based on the type of flower and its color, say whatever comes into your mind. You may reveal what could be happening in your friend's life at present or in the future.

❊ Close your eyes while holding the flower. You may see a different color in your mind. Interpret the significance of that color as well as any other colors you see.

❊ **Clairsentience: *feeling with the mind and body.***

With your eyes open or closed, use clairsentience to feel the flower. A flower with a long stem may tell you that the person whose flower you are holding could be going on a long journey. You may feel the stem is suggesting a motorway or an airstrip.

The leaves may indicate that your friend is going to a building or a room. How the leaves feel can suggest whether they are alone or in company, apprehensive, or happy. Feel the leaves to sense and see what type of building or room your friend may soon be visiting. The number of leaves may help you to feel when the event may occur. Say whatever comes into your mind because first inclinations are the ones to follow.

Long narrow leaves could indicate a tall building; shiny leaves, that the building has a lot of plate glass windows. Furry leaves could hint at comfort; and prickly leaves may predict uncomfortable surroundings or difficult people.

Smell the flower to see what the present or future may hold in store for your friend. The scent may suggest the sea or countryside, a restaurant, or someone's home.

Its perfume may bring a taste to your tongue. You will

need to interpret it as nice or nasty, at home or abroad. The flower's smell may suggest a certain food or country.

※ **Clairaudience:** *spirit voices.*

Use clairaudience, the ability to hear sounds that are usually inaudible. Just as you can recall a conversation that you had with someone yesterday, you may hear *spirit voices* in your mind that haven't actually been spoken. Say out loud what you are hearing because it will probably be relevant to the person whose fortune you are telling.

※ When giving a flower reading, use your knowledge of flowers and color as well as your five senses of sight, touch, smell, hearing, and taste. The combination of these five senses is your intuition, or sixth sense.

※ When you have finished telling your friend's flower fortune, say who you think brought the flower. Then read the flower fortunes of your other guests.

CHAPTER
5

Wishes For Love

Romany Flower Love Wishes
Rosalo Kamipen Chovihoni Booti

The loveliness in every flower is an expression of love.
Lovers give bouquets of flowers to woo their sweethearts.
Just as a flower is a miracle, so love is a miracle. You can
make miracles happen by using flowers according to the
beliefs Romanies have about flowers and other plants. You
can make a wish to help love come into your life. Your
aspiration is more than the longings of your imagination; it
is a prophecy of what will happen in the future.

When you cast a wish, it is a way of helping what you
have been longing for to come true. Your thought goes into
the ether, the clear heavenly air that is all around us. Once
you have made your wish, keep it a secret, forget about it,

and have faith that it will be granted.

Here are some of the rituals that Romanies use when they make a wish for love.

To Reveal Who Loves You Most

You may be in a quandary because you have two admirers and you can't choose between them. You know you can't have them both. Romanies tackle the problem with the help of an onion.

♥ Take an onion for each admirer. Use a pin to score each onion with the initial of one of the admirers.

♥ Leave the onions in a warm place, balanced in the neck of a jar of water. The first onion to sprout green shoots reveals which admirer is more fond of you. If the onions shoot at the same time, plant them in a pot or in the garden. The onion that blooms first will reveal the admirer who is more deserving of your affections.

To Hold on to Love

If you want your love to last forever, try this.

♥ Make a Plasticine model of yourself and the one you love. Give them details, such as your hairstyles and the type of clothes you each wear.

♥ Place a rose, which represents love and embodies mystic thoughts, on the image of the boy.

♥ Put the figures face to face with their arms around each

other and with the rose between them. Wrap them in a handkerchief and place them in a new envelope.

♥ Hide the envelope in a drawer. Do not open the envelope, unless you wish to finish the relationship.

♥ If you decide that the relationship has run its course, open the envelope, remove the rose, roll the Plasticine into a ball, and bury all three of them together.

To Have Love Returned

If your sweetheart's attention appears to be fading, he or she forgets to call at the promised time, and no longer tries to please you when you are together, then it's time to make a love wish.

♥ Pick or buy a flower that you feel represents your sweetheart. Stay outside or sit at a window with the flower in your hand. Stare into the sky until you find a cloud with which you feel an affinity.

♥ Ask the cloud to please carry a message from you to the one you desire. Close your eyes for a few moments and concentrate on your wish.

♥ Turn away from the cloud before you open your eyes. Do not look at the cloud again because to do so will drag your wish back to earth. Place the flower in a vase next to your bed. Before the flower dies your sweetheart should show some response.

To Keep an Unwanted Boyfriend Away

You no longer like your boyfriend and wish he would leave you in peace. But he will not take all the subtle hints you have been giving out, and he's being a pest. This wish might help.

✘ On the night of a full moon, write his name on a small piece of new paper, then fold it so his name is not visible.

✘ In daylight, bury the paper under some stinging nettles which are ruled by Mars, the planet that represents male passion.

✘ As the moon wanes (gets smaller) and the paper disintegrates in the soil, so will your admirer's interest in you fade away.

✘ Because Venus embodies female passion, a boy trying to get rid of a girl should write her name on a fresh piece of paper and bury it under a bramble because the blackberry bush is ruled by Venus.

To Win the Heart of the One You Desire

If you are longing in vain for someone to notice you, perhaps it's time to make this love wish.

♥ On a Friday, which is ruled by the love planet Venus, keep the one you love in mind as you pick or buy two roses. Think of your beloved as you place the roses together in a vase that has no other flowers or foliage in it.

♥ Place the vase beside your bed, on your dressing table or desk, or wherever else you feel is the best place for the flowers.

♥ When the roses fade, remove them from the water. Light a candle, then write your name and his or hers on a piece of new paper. Draw a heart around them. Now place the faded roses in an envelope with the paper and make your wish. Seal the envelope to keep in the wish. Blow out the candle.

♥ Sleep with the envelope under your pillow until the full moon. After which you should keep the envelope in a drawer where it will remain undisturbed.

♥ When you have won the heart of the one you desire, bury the envelope without opening it.

CHAPTER 6

Back to the Future

You now know many of the Romany secrets of tea-leaf reading, the language of flowers, and how to make wishes come true. The time has come for you to impress your friends with your uncanny sense of their desires for love and success, and their hopes for the future.

Put the white cups on the table and open a fresh packet of tea. If you are having a barbecue, set up a lantern or candles so you have plenty of light to read the tea leaves and/or flowers. Add to the Romany atmosphere by playing passionate, romantic Gypsy music. Ask each of your friends to bring a flower. After their reading, pop the flower into a vase and make a wish for harmonious friendship.

Remember, reading fortunes is kid's stuff because children are often very intuitive. You are sure to be a huge success and before long will be hearing how you amaze people with your predictions. If it becomes your hobby or regular party trick, you will surprise even yourself with the accuracy of your predictions. Being able to foretell the future and read people's character will be a positive asset throughout your life.

There is a knock at the door. Your friends have arrived, put the kettle on. Good luck.

Kushti bok as the Romanies would wish you.